# MOON TIDE

CAPE COD POEMS

## *Also by Mary Petiet*

Wash Ashore

Cape Cod: A Writer's Journal

Owl Magic: Your Guide Through Challenging Times

Minerva's Owls

# MOON TIDE

## CAPE COD POEMS

MARY PETIET

Sea Crow Press
*amplifying voices*

*Moon Tide: Cape Cod Poems*
Sea Crow Press


ISBN Ebook 978-0-578648-16-3
ISBN Paperback 978-0-578646-60-2
Library of Congress Control Number: 2020908868

Front Cover Image © Mary Petiet, Cover Designed by PopKitty
Author Photo by Kate Shelter
Interior Photography by Mary Petiet
Interior Formatting by Mary Petiet

www.seacrowpress.com

*For Daisy*

# Contents

# SUMMER POEMS

## Black Dog

Black Dog spends hours
staring into tide pools
and explodes the briny minnow-verse
pouncing on the darting minnow shadows.

The sun climbs the sky
and inches down again,
Black Dog has no need of a watch.

Black Dog lives entirely
in the moment now
running the beach with no thought
of later and before,
no what if no regret,
only Black Dog beach and sky
the eternal now, now, now.

## Minister Emeritus

The last time I heard the Minister Emeritus
the church on the hill
was sticky hot with July heat,
and he delivered his sermon,
which really wasn't a sermon
in a measured age-soft voice,
and held us in his wise-warm watery gaze.

And as we rose to leave the sanctuary
the pianist tapped gently
the opening strains
of American in Paris,
and we started moving
down the aisle
of the Unitarian church,
gently swaying,
as close as we could come
to dancing
in the Unitarian church.

And the pianist played
more boldly
as the Gershwin started
swinging
and we were swung aloft
on rays of sunshine

as the Minister Emeritus gently smiled
goodbye to each of us
as we passed outside the church.

## Hermit Crab

Low tide finds Hermit Crab
safely snug in his hermitage,
the idea of tiny houses
seems not so very new,
at least at the bottom
of the summer tide pool.

Hermit Crab lives the hermit life
in his portable shell for one,
and I wonder if he thinks
in streams of poetry such isolation breeds,

and does he trace his songs
across the sand slowly
as he travels the low tide flats
away from dangerous boys
with pails and poking sticks?

## Poseidon's Museum

A pale wooden cask
poked from a sand flat
the morning after a gale

so I spent half the day's low tide
digging around it inventing stories
about what it had held:
Molasses, rum, jewels,
and gold bullion,
until the tide came pouring in.

The water rose
as I salvaged just one hole plug
and jumped back on the skiff
to float away on the rushing tide,
and next tide the cask was gone.

Poseidon keeps
a whimsical museum,
and only shares his collection occasionally.

## Sailing

The boy tacks away from shore
following the pier's reach to the sea.

Confident astern
he grasps tiller and main
as the sail fills with wind
and his hair glows golden
in the morning sun.
He glides past pier's end into the deep.

I want to call him back,
but hold my peace,
and he sails straight and true
joining the other racing boats
headed to the start line
near the channel, close to the ferries.

The race clusters there together
waiting on the start horn,
and I lose sight of his bright hair
as it blends into the boat-crowded,
breeze-kissed summer haze.

Sailing is freedom.
He is captain of his own boat,
alone upon his small floating universe.

Sailing
is independence
self-reliance, and pure faith.

Our Cape Cod village
harbors many sailors of varied age
and experience,
and as new sailors raise sails
old salts lower theirs,
de-rigging slowly,
riding the sea's rhythm
as long as they may,
reluctant to give up
the salt, the spray, the challenge.

And as they de-rig,
they share their experience
and a priceless body
of sea-knowledge is passed
generation to generation to generation.

A sailboat is rarely empty
and a mooring, never.
I imagine an empty sailboat
brings bad luck,
and see far too few moorings
to allow the luxury of disuse.

As old salts age from the sea,
they pass not only
their stories and experience,
but even their very boats
to the next generation
that they may sail on
one day without them.

We are pushed by the wind
and followed by the sea
in a motley assortment of boats
that are a part of our community,
boats that have sailed
through the years
and generations,
known as old friends
with distinct personalities
racing, teaching,
and cruising the harbor.

This summer
we have a beautiful Rhodes 19,
a lovely vintage vessel
dating to 1975.
She was generously
passed on to us
by a friend who got too old,
and each time we sail,
a bit of him sails with us.

The Rhodes rides
on my dad's old mooring,
which he signed over to me
when he could no longer manage it.

The wheel turns, and time passes.
The hand on the tiller changes,
but the boat plies on,
and the eight-year-old sailing
past the dock out of reach
forms a new knot in a long line.

# FALL POEMS

## Four Feathers

The morning came
with an offering
of four fine grey feathers
just inside the door
beside the usual mudroom jumble
of shoes and coats and sports gear,

a tiny offering,
all that was left of the bird
flown aloft in the cold dawn light
and eaten before full sunrise

by a black contented cat,
who has never known hunger
and kills because
his nature is to kill.

## Scots Grey

Finally, the beach is quiet.
Late October grey
rides a tilting autumn axis, filling the sky
with shadows I have seen
riding the Scottish sky
three thousand miles away.

Sunshine crosses the water
to the lighthouse,
and windy fluid Scottish weather
covers my sandy Cape Cod shore.

The Black Dog and I
have the beach to ourselves,
and the reliable tide,
driven by a sharp northeast wind,
overflows the beach.

The harbor looks swollen
nearly all high tides this fall
so we walk up to surer footing
and meet no one.

And the wind sings
through tall brown reeds,
and we are observed
by empty staring windows
and sheltering birds,

and we are blown
by that sharp clean wind
in the solitary freedom
brought each fall
by grey-clothed time
and the quiet shift
of the seasonal wheel.

## Beach Debris

Beer can, bottle top, ballpoint pen
cigarettes, candy-wrapper, chip bag.

Beach debris deposited by a
moon tide
on a strong northeast wind.
We flip trash from the wrack line
into a found two-gallon drum
with handle, marked Kikkoman.

Flip flop, boat shoe, sneaker
fishing line, rusted hooks,
shellfish license, clothes,
gear from the oyster grants

*Don't those oyster guys say*
*they're cleaning the harbor?*
*What is NOT on the beach?*
My ten year old asks
as we gather debris
while the Black Dog runs the flats.

Plastic, plywood, PVC
ribbons, rope, balloons
zip lock, single-use plastic bags.

*Someday we'll find something really great,*
*mom,* says the boy.

The dog flits glossy black
through the late October light,
I see the boy glowing blond
and think *there it is.*

## Labor Day Seagull

An entire summer passed
with barely a seagull insight
A few distant on the flats,
a few on the dock, a few.

Were they avoiding the
inevitable crowds suddenly shy,
or were they fading from view
with the other creatures so quietly
leaving our world forever?

I wandered all summer
among boaters delighted
by clean decks and white sails,
relieved to avoid the bird dropped mess.

After Labor Day the crowds left
and I went down to the water
and the missing birds
were all lined up
on the boardwalk railing,
a riot of color and noise
and droppings,
a Hitchcockian scene,
a bird reunion,
white and mottled seagulls,
a few majestic cormorants,
a host of terns a-flutter.

The noise was terrific
and the was smell high
with their funky chalky foulness
coating every surface.

Suddenly one bright seagull
swooped down low
bringing up a quahog,
to hover on a wind current
and hurl his prize to earth

and a universe shattered on the rocks.

## Homecoming

An insistent voice calls *hello!*
outside my door,
a voice unrecognizable
in everything but its urgency.

I open the door.
Silence.
No breeze, no birdsong
the autumn evening
shadows gather
and there is no man
claiming that strong voice.

The New England house is old.
It dates to the 1840s officially
but has evidence
of far greater age.

An entire tree of a girth now unseen
supports the west end of the house
from north to south,
hewn by an adze, fossilized in whale oil.

An ancient well
is buried
in the depths
beneath
the living room.

Ancient headstones
lurk
beneath the porch.

Rewiring the empty house
on a twilit summer evening
the electrician heard someone
calling him outside,
and running to see who it was
found only silence.

Inside he heard a woman's tread wearing
the floorboards upstairs
always the same spot,
always pacing,
in the day's dusky
in-between time.

He never saw her
but named her The Walker,
and told me,
*She's walkin', oh, yes she's walkin'*
*and waitin',*
and turned back
to his work rewiring.

Sometimes in New England
past and present merge,
and the living
coexist with the dead.

My old school bus driver
visits the neighbor across the street
in a house
even older than mine.
The two embody history,
180 years
counted all-together.

I ask them about my house,
the old house called
Moonstone
for the white round quartz
set in the front stone wall
that really does look like
the man in the moon.

*In 1923 a man drove his car*
*clear through the back of your barn.*
*Through the wall.*
*Dropped down 20 feet.*
*Meant to reverse out,*
*but went forward,*
*straight through instead.*
*Ohh, he was alright, but the car wasn't.*

The corpse of a Model T
rests behind my back stone wall,
in many rusted pieces.

*A boy lived in your house,*
*early 1920s.*
*He was young,*
*about twenty years old.*
*Fitted the gauge of his*
*truck to match*
*the rail tracks outback*
*to bring his gear*
*to work the cranberry bog*
*beyond the tracks more easy.*
*One day the train came in fast and*
*killed him. Never came home,*
*long as his mother waited.*

Another early summer evening.
This call from the porch,
and this time my six-year-old
hears it with me,
and together we run to see
what is so urgent.

Complete silence.
I act on instinct.

*Hello Man, welcome,*
*please come in!*

I throw the porch door wide.

*You're welcome home anytime,*
*Hello Man.*

I have named him
and welcomed him home.

The walker is still now,
the calls of hello silent.

# WINTER POEMS

## Deep Freeze

It got so cold the harbor froze
beneath gunmetal skies,
and the ice cracked
and the Black Dog stood out in stark relief
against the whiteness of it all,
finding frozen schoolies
along the icy wrack line,
to carry proudly up the iced-in beach
cold between her warm-sharp teeth.

The black ducks stood out
in their own small relief
and found no open water,
yet the ice was treacherous and held
no weight
and the icebergs piled higher
and even the channel froze
and it was as if the very Ice Age
had returned.

Once the Black Dog ventured
far out onto the ice
and hearing it shift and crack,
and fearing it would break
I called her back to safety.

## Stone Walls

The farmhouse enjoyed
an ocean view,
before the bleating livestock
all moved west
and the tall brush forest
choked the fields
between the water
and the windows.

The land was hard to farm
through the clay and the rocks,
and now it seems hardly soil
and hardly farming at all.

But the old farmhouse
stands sturdy
beside the silent barn,
built to last and lasting
within the old stone walls,
reliable grey-stone
English hedgerows
built an ocean from home,
stone veins tracing the landscape
in a network of farmer's anchors,
heavy and sure
to outlast other traces
of that hard farm life.

When Cape Cod
finally slips beneath the waves,
the old stone anchors
will continue marking
old boundaries
at the bottom of the sea,
explored by fish
and colonized by mussels.

## Old Cedar

Old cedar knows why growing
into the wind is certainly
no solution.
It tried once, and proof of the
attempt lingers in the twisted
gray trunk
below a shock of green
on branches curved
by the forceful old south wind.

Old cedar stands a lonely figure
defying the wind
as relentless ocean water
comes ever closer
slowly claiming it from below.

## Storm Bird

My father as a young man
braved a blizzard's wake
and found a snowy owl
frozen in the surf.

Almost lost, a brave storm bird
too majestic to abandon,
he gathered it cold and lifeless,
wishing it warm and quick.

A taxidermist granted his whim.

And the smoothed white feathers
became forever unruffled,
the smooth white wings
forever folded,
the keen black eyes
forever open,
and the brave storm bird
forever alive, but not.

## New England Hades

The goat died in a snow-bound
mid-winter field
sometime between
dusk and dawn.

There is no marker.

The days were short
when the goat died,
and the farmer had tended them
late as the afternoon sun
set cold and bright
between trees to the west.

I saw him there,
and he handed me a gallon
of warm, foamy milk
from his herd.

The farmer and his wife
were new to Cape Cod
and had come to farmland
newly reopened for agriculture.

Theirs were the first goats seen
on these fields in generations,
and they were excitedly
producing milk.

I fed my small children the milk,
and they grew strong-boned
and healthy.
I made yogurt and cheese,
I utilized the whey
and befriended the curds.

Everything looked fine that dusk,
but the morning light revealed
the one dead goat.

Born too small, too soon, too cold.

New England winter knows
a rare dull fury.
The cold Hades of the ancients
could be New England fields
buried in snow,
ponds iced over, winds howling.

It is no time to be born.

# SPRING POEMS

## Moon Tide

I've only seen the deepest secret
part of the harbor once
when a full moon tide
pulled the water out

and I stood

before the sandy point
deep in the channel's hidden canyon,
in a cool damp
water world

where a ribbon of blue three feet wide
lay enchanted by the moon.

I almost leapt across
but didn't dare
for fear of falling in.

## Tree Man

A mighty tree stood dying
on the courthouse lawn,
but its demise was not official
until the local tree man's declaration,
after long consultation
with the tree itself.

Once the tree man told
me how he sees the trees.

Sentient on earth, anchored to ground
reaching for the sky each one connected.

The tree man found, after consultation,
that the courthouse tree was dying,
and he found that it comfortably housed
a family of young raccoons.

Most people trap raccoons
and drown them in the harbor.
But that is not the tree man's way.

Instead, he conversed with the tree
and the raccoons
and before any deadly declarations,
before a single saw was honed,
before the raccoons could
even wonder,
the tree man gently moved them
to a new and healthy tree.

## Crab Nebula

A celestial crab
inhabits the constellation Taurus,
At home in a starburst remnant
of celestial debris,
the crab nebula is perhaps
protected by the bull.

Didn’t Carl Sagan say
we all are made of starstuff
and doesn't that apply
to even the humble ancient
horseshoe crab,
Earth’s archaic blue blood,
living relic of an old lost world?

Horseshoe crab watched dinosaurs
rise and fall,
horseshoe crab survived the comet impact
in the depths of the cool mud.
Horseshoe crab survived everything,
except perhaps man.

For there is no hiding from man,
and Taurus does not
protect horseshoe crab
as it enacts the ancient crab ritual,
crawling ashore on the late spring tide to mate
as the crab nebula is obscured
from view in our northeastern sky
by bright midsummer's light.

Each year there are fewer
horseshoe crabs,
stardust and timelessness
can't stop them being used for chum
and beaches where the sand
was once covered
by scores of hoary-ugly
tourist-terrifying horseshoe crabs
are now bare on full spring tides
with clean, unmarked sand.

## Four Hundred Bulbs

I imagine the grief-struck
heading into the storm
armed with shovel and trowel,
soaked by cold wind-driven rain,
clutching four hundred bulbs
of promised spring blossom.

I imagine them digging deep
into the wet earth
of my aunt's memorial garden,
burying bulbs
not far from the grave
where we buried half her ashes
last summer
after scattering the rest
from the highest dune
on the beach
under the blue sky
the blue of her eye
the blue of the far horizon
where all blues merge endlessly
in endless blue haze.

I imagine she watches
the hungry ground
receive the bulbs
and knows the vivid vital promise
of spring's eternal return.

## Rock

Rock sits the size of a Mini-Cooper
in my front yard
along the Old King's Highway,
and that's just the part you can see.

For all I know,
Rock goes deep into the earth
possibly emerging in China,
and right now a Chinese writer
is puzzling out a story
about this immovable rock
occupying prime real estate
on her own front lawn.

23,000 years ago Cape Cod
was born of an ice sheet.

The receding ice
left the long arm of the Cape
jutting into the cold Atlantic
piled with rocks, lined with scars
pocked with kettle holes
brimming icy afterbirth.

We live atop a scene of ancient devastation.

The noise of all those tons
of moving rock and ice
must have been deafening,
but today I hear
the springtime chirp of tree frogs,
emerging from hibernation
deep within the loamy depths
of the kettle hole near Rock.

A pair of ducks return here annually
with ducklings in mind,
quiet hatching to counter
the land's ancient booming.

I sit on Rock warm in the spring sun
feeling the ages
feeling the energy flowing through Rock
as surely as it flows
through us all in mute connection.

Can Rock remember the primeval time
before man came to our narrow land,
time of saber tooth tigers
wandering the sand flats,
the time of unrecognizable beasts
dotting the surf?

Then the time of the first people,
wanderers from beyond the Bering Strait
probing south and east
for good game and fishing and settling
to establish a footpath past Rock.

Soft moccasined feet passed Rock,
until suddenly leather boots
traversed the beaten dirt
and the path widened into a road,
and horses and wagons joined the traffic.

Booted people built my house
and still Rock sat too big to move,
ensconced between the house and the road
watching the people glean a hard-won life
from inhospitable soil.

Miles of stone walls were built
from smaller movable rocks,
each pulled painfully from
the earth by teams of oxen,
and still Rock watched
as farmers switched to sheep
for an easier living.

Pavement was laid
and phone poles raised
and street lights began greeting the dusk,
and Rock suddenly no longer knew
true dark, and tried to remember
true black night.

Now Rock knows
summer traffic and winter plows,
the daily school bus and the paperboy.
Rock knows us.
Does Rock remember?

Sitting upon Rock in the spring warmth,
I remember.

# About the Author

Mary Petiet is an author, poet, and publisher. In 2020 she founded Sea Crow Press. A long-time contributor to *Edible Cape Cod Magazine,* Mary is also the author of *Wash Ashore*, *Cape Cod: A Writer's Journal*, *Owl Magic,* and *Minerva's Owls*. Her work is frequently inspired by her native Cape Cod, where she can sometimes be found wandering the marsh in all weather.

# Sea Crow Press

Sea Crow Press is named for a flock of five talkative crows you can find on the beach anywhere between Scudder Lane and Bone Hill Road in Barnstable Village on Cape Cod.

According to Norse legend, one-eyed Odin sent two crows out into the world so they could return and tell him its stories. If you sit and listen to the sea crows in Barnstable as they fly and roost and chatter, it's an easy legend to believe.

Operating from the premise that the small press plays an essential part in contemporary arts by amplifying its voices, Sea Crow Press is committed to building an accessible community of writers and dedicated to telling stories that matter.

www.seacrowpress.com